R. C. (Robert Cassie) Waterston

Tribute to William Cullen Bryant

R. C. (Robert Cassie) Waterston

Tribute to William Cullen Bryant

ISBN/EAN: 9783743311923

Manufactured in Europe, USA, Canada, Australia, Japa

Cover: Foto ©ninafisch / pixelio.de

Manufactured and distributed by brebook publishing software
(www.brebook.com)

R. C. (Robert Cassie) Waterston

Tribute to William Cullen Bryant

RESOLUTIONS.

Resolved, By the Massachusetts Historical Society, that in the death of our distinguished Honorary Member, WILLIAM CULLEN BRYANT, our country has lost a patriotic and noble citizen, the press an accomplished and powerful journalist, and American literature one of its earliest, purest, and most enduring ornaments.

Resolved, That while we remember with pride that he was born in Massachusetts, and educated at one of our own colleges, our warmest sympathies in this bereavement are due, and are hereby offered, to the scholars and to the whole people of New York, with whom he has been so long and so eminently associated, and to whom his genius and his fame have been ever so justly dear.

Resolved, That these Resolutions be communicated to the New York Historical Society, with the assurance that our hearts are with them in lamenting the loss, and in doing honor to the memory, of their illustrious associate and vice-president.

Resolved, That a Committee of five be appointed by the chair to represent this Society at the funeral of Mr. Bryant.

THE RESOLUTIONS WERE SECONDED BY THE

REV. R. C. WATERSTON,

AT THE CLOSE OF WHOSE REMARKS THEY WERE ADOPTED, AND THE PRESIDENT APPOINTED AS THE COMMITTEE TO ATTEND MR. BRYANT'S FUNERAL,

PROFESSOR HENRY W. LONGFELLOW.

PROFESSOR OLIVER WENDELL HOLMES.

REV. ROBERT C. WATERSTON.

HON. RICHARD FROTHINGHAM.

MR. DELANO A. GODDARD.

REMARKS OF REV. R. C. WATERSTON.

IT is difficult to express the sense of loss which comes to us in the death of William Cullen Bryant. He has so long been the object of our veneration and love, that he seemed to have become an essential part of our life. Few of us can remember when his name did not stand pre-eminent in our literature. It is now more than sixty years since his "Thanatopsis" was published, which at once gained a reputation that has never since been questioned. From that time, his active public career has kept his name constantly before the community, and always on the side of patriotism, justice, and humanity. With an inflexible purpose, he has vindicated what he felt to be right. Whatever seemed to him connected with the best interests of humanity was dear to his heart. There was hardly an enterprise associated with human progress with which his name had not become identified. Venerable in age, he still had the fresh energy of youth; and, though he had arrived at a period of life when most men feel that they may retire from active service, he sought no relaxation from duty, he asked no exemption from the weight of personal responsibility. With breadth of thought and profoundness of conviction, he could adapt himself to the immediate wants of the time, bringing to each occasion what was most needed. Thus, when from the midst of such activity he has been suddenly taken away, it is as if a guiding star had been stricken from the firmament.

Mr. Bryant was a scholar, yet his life was not passed either in studious retirement, or even, in a scholastic way, among books. He was familiar with various languages, ancient and modern, retaining with critical exactness his classical knowledge, yet his hours were habitually occupied with the practical business of the time, political economy, finance, and the changing aspects of national affairs. He was an ardent lover of Nature, yet his days were, for the most part, associated with the crowded thoroughfares of a populous city. His poetry was generally calm and contemplative, yet he was in daily contact with the most exciting controversies of the period, the contentions of conflicting parties, and the agitating questions that threatened to disturb communities, and even to divide the Nation. It was not so much what he was in any one phase of his character, as in the perfect balance of all his powers, the manner in which every faculty was brought into harmonious action, and the noble spirit with which they were uniformly and persistently devoted to the public good.

We may have had elsewhere as faithful citizens; as industrious journalists; as ripe scholars;—and poets, it may be, equally gifted and inspired, but where have we had another who has combined in his own person all these? In him a rare combination of extraordinary qualities was united; — strength and gentleness; elevation of thought and childlike simplicity; genius, common-sense, and practical wisdom. Where there were controverted questions, whether men agreed with him or not, they never for an instant doubted his nobleness of purpose. It was universally acknowledged that his integrity was as immovable as a mountain of adamant; and that, in all his efforts, he had no motive less elevated than the public good.

Bryant, the acknowledged pioneer, lived to become also the patriarch, in our world of letters; while those who have entered the field at a later day, and have since risen to a world-wide reputation, have never been reluctant to do him homage. Familiar as he has been with the literature of other countries, no one could mistake the nationality of his writings. As there are fruits which take their flavor from the soil in which they grow, so what he has written, by its bloom and aroma, testifies to the land of its birth. Not only the legends and traditions of his country, but its scenery and spirit, through him have become familiar. He has identified himself with our fields and forests. The sky, the stream, and the prairie, speak of him. The winds whisper his name, and in the crowded street he is remembered. The gentian and the violet ever blend the thought of him with their fragrance. Seed-time and harvest, summer and winter, sing his praises. The very freshness of Nature comes to us in all he wrote. The breath of the woods, the atmosphere of the hills, the light of the sun and the stars, are interwoven with his spirit. His love, his hope, his faith, his exalted thought, his rapt devotion, are identified with them all.

While I speak, I am carried back in thought to pleasant days enjoyed with Mr. Bryant at Heidelberg. As we walked together under the shadow of the " Rent Tower ; " in the famous garden of " Elizabeth," wife of the Count Palatine ; and along the " Terrace," which commands one of the most magnificent views in Europe, I felt that, admirable as were the choicest of Mr. Bryant's productions, he was himself far more than the best that had proceeded from his pen. In him there was robust nobleness, with quiet repose ; variety and completeness ; intuitive insight, and affluence of knowledge. Not under any circumstance was there the faintest approach to ostentation or display, but as occasion required, all needed information was at hand, and always in the most agreeable manner. Whatever else there was, you were sure of substantial reality. Mr. Bryant was a man of close observation and exactness. With regard to trees and plants, he had the accuracy of a naturalist. The history and character of every shrub were familiar to him, while with these was a sense of beauty and harmony that quivered through his whole being, an emotion all the deeper because of its calmness. Outward objects were reflected from his mind like images in a tranquil lake, but not like those destined to pass away. He absorbed them, and they became his own. His eye embraced every thing;—the stupendous ruin, the winding river, the encircling mountains, the motion of birds, their varied songs, the clouds sailing through the heavens, and each floating shadow on the landscape. Nothing escaped him.

Both at Heidelberg and along the Neckar, we climbed the hills, wandering among ancient castles and picturesque ruins, and bringing away memories never to be forgotten. I felt then, as I do now, that no man living could be more keenly alive to the most delicate aspects of external nature; or could interpret, with truer wisdom, her hidden meaning.

I had the privilege also of being with Mr. Bryant at Naples. He first showed me the grave of Virgil. We looked from that beautiful city out over its world-renowned Bay. I listened to his inspiring words upon Italy, for whose progressive future he cherished an unfailing hope. But there were other thoughts which pressed upon his mind. Mrs. Bryant, who was journeying with him, had become suddenly prostrated by serious illness. He had watched over her through many anxious weeks. This cloud, which had thrown its ominous shadow over his pathway, seemed now lifting, and bursts of sunshine filled his heart with joy. At this time, April 23, 1858, I received from him a note, stating that there was a subject of interest upon which he would like to converse with me. On the following day, the weather being delightful, we walked in the "Villa Reale," the royal park or garden over-looking the Bay of Naples. Never can I forget the beautiful spirit that breathed through every word he uttered, the reverent love, the confiding trust, the aspiring hope, the deep-rooted faith. Every thought, every view, was generous and comprehensive. Anxiously watching, as he had been doing, in that twilight boundary between this world and another, over one more precious to him than life itself, the divine truths and promises had come home to his mind with new power. He stated that he had never united himself with the Church, which with his present feelings he would most gladly do. He then asked if it would be agreeable to me to come to his room on the morrow and administer the Communion, adding that, as he had not been baptized, he desired that ordinance at the same time. The day following was the Sabbath, and a most heavenly day. In fulfilment of his wishes, in his own quiet room, a company of seven persons celebrated together the Lord's Supper. With hymns, selection from the Scripture, and devotional exercises, we went back in thought to the "large upper room," where Christ first instituted the Holy Supper in the midst of his Disciples. Previous to the breaking of bread, William Cullen Bryant was baptized. With snow-white head and flowing beard, he stood like one of the ancient Prophets, and perhaps never since the days of the Apostles has a truer disciple professed allegiance to the Divine Master.

Had he not this very hour of the Holy Communion in his thought, when, in his later published Poems (embracing in spiritual sympathy the whole Christian Church), he speaks of —

> " The consecrated bread, —
> The mystic loaf that crowns the board,
> When, round the table of their Lord,
> Within a thousand temples set,
> In memory of the bitter death
> Of Him who taught at Nazareth,
> His followers are met,
> And thoughtful eyes with tears are wet,
> As of the Holy One they think,
> The glory of whose rising, yet
> Makes bright the grave's mysterious brink."

2

After the service, while standing at the window, looking out with Mr. Bryant over the Bay, smooth as glass, (the same water over which the Apostle Paul sailed, in the ship from Alexandria, when he brought Christianity into Italy), the graceful outline of the Island of Capri relieved against the sky, — with that glorious scene reposing before us, Mr. Bryant repeated the lines of John Leyden, the Oriental scholar and poet ; lines which, he said, had always been special favorites of his, and of which he was often reminded by that holy tranquillity which seems, as with conscious recognition, to characterize the Lord's Day.

> "With silent awe, I hail the sacred morn,
> That scarcely wakes while all the fields are still;
> A soothing calm on every breeze is borne,
> A graver murmur echoes from the hill,
> And softer sings the linnet from the thorn.
> Hail, light serene! Hail, sacred Sabbath morn ! "

Never did poet have a truer companion, a sincerer spiritual helpmate than did Mr. Bryant in his wife. Refined in taste, and elevated in thought, she was characterized alike by goodness and gentleness. Modest in herself, she lived wholly for him. His welfare, his happiness, his fame, were the chief objects of her ambition. To smooth his pathway, to cheer his spirit, to harmonize every discordant element of life, were purposes for the accomplishment of which no sacrifice on her part could be too great. And nothing could surpass the devotion which he extended to her, as marked to the very close of her life, as in the first year of their union. Never did Dante or Petrarch love more profoundly, or pay more immortal homage to the object of their love.

In the early freshness of her youthful bloom, Mr. Bryant had sung : —

> "Thy sports, thy wanderings, when a child,
> Were ever in the sylvan wild;
> And all the beauty of the place
> Is in thy heart and on thy face.

> The forest depths, by foot unpressed,
> Are not more sinless than thy breast;
> The holy peace, that fills the air
> Of those calm solitudes, is there."

Where in the whole history of literature can be found a more exquisite tribute than that paid to her in his lines on the " Future Life " ?

> " How shall I know thee in the sphere which keeps
> The disembodied spirits of the dead?
>
> For I shall feel the sting of ceaseless pain
> If there I meet thy gentle presence not;
> Nor hear the voice I love, nor read again
> In thy serenest eyes the tender thought."

On her recovery from illness at Naples, Mr. Bryant wrote the touching lines on " The Life that is."

> Thou, who so long hast pressed the couch of pain,
> Oh welcome, welcome back to life's free breath; —
> To life's free breath and day's sweet light again,
> From the chill shadows of the gate of death!
>
> Twice wert thou given me; once in thy fair prime,
> Fresh from the fields of youth, when first we met,
> And all the blossoms of that hopeful time
> Clustered and glowed where'er thy steps were set ;
>
> And now, in thy ripe autumn, once again
> Given back to fervent prayers and yearnings strong,
> From the drear realm of sickness and of pain
> When we had watched, and feared, and trembled long.
>
> Now may we keep thee from the balmy air
> And radiant walks of heaven a little space,
> Where He, who went before thee to prepare
> For His meek followers, shall assign thy place.

Since Mr. Bryant's return to this country, now twenty years ago, I have had pleasant intercourse with him, both at Roslyn and Cummington, seeing him in the quiet enjoyment of home, surrounded by his family and amid the delightful companionship of books. Nowhere did Mr. Bryant appear more attractive; his hearty cordiality and genial manners making every one feel at ease, while his conversation, both natural and playful, sparkled with brilliancy; serious and weighty when occasion required, and overflowing with merriment when that was in season. Never was he more charming than when, throwing aside formal reserve, he would relate with a glow of humor pleasant incidents, bringing, with graphic power, each scene depicted vividly before his hearers. On such occasions he would at times reproduce the voice and manner of others with an ability absolutely startling; Wordsworth, Rogers, Combe, Webster, seemed to be in your presence; so individual were the accents, you could hardly believe it was not themselves speaking.

One day at Roslyn he appeared in the full dress obtained at Damascus, slippers, turban, and flowing robes; when, seating himself after the manner of the East, he gave an interesting account of his experience in Syria and Palestine. Fortunate would have been the artist who could have transferred the scene to canvas! At different times he repeated poems of which he was the author, in a low melodious voice, revealing often, with gentle emphasis, unexpected depths of meaning. In such recitations there seemed no effort of memory. The thought was not something apart from himself, but a living portion of his nature, through which his life throbbed. Perhaps no one, who has not thus heard them, can fully comprehend their true vitality.

At Cummington, the place of his birth, it was deeply interesting to go with him over scenes associated with his early days. He showed me the spot where the school-house stood, in which he learned his first lessons; and the grassy bank over whose green slope he remembered to have romped and rolled when a child. We visited together the "Rivulet"

" whose waters drew
His little feet when life was new."

Here also were felt his earliest poetic impulses,

> " Duly I sought thy banks, and tried
> My first rude numbers by thy side."

We wandered about, over those beautiful regions, day after day ; and, as memories of the past thronged upon Mr. Bryant's mind, it was a rare pleasure to listen to such reminiscences. We sought out the lonely spot associated with the " Two Graves," while he related the strange tradition connected with the place. We walked also into the " Entrance to a Wood,"

> " where the thick roof
> Of green and stirring branches was alive
> And musical with birds."

We were at " the old homestead," where Mr. Bryant was born, and where he passed all his younger days, remaining into early manhood. His father was well known here as the " Beloved Physician." The place for some years had been out of the family, and Mr. Bryant was very happy in the thought that he had come into possession of it again. He had rebuilt the mansion, and made various improvements, saving whatever could be saved, and especially preserving all the old landmarks. His own words describe precisely the general aspect of the country : —

> " I stood upon the upland slope, and cast
> Mine eye upon a broad and beauteous scene,
> Where the vast plain lay girt by mountains vast,
> And hills o'er hills lifted their heads of green,
> With pleasant vales scooped out, and villages between."

He mentioned that while studying law with Judge Howe, the Judge was greatly concerned when he found him reading a volume of Wordsworth, fearing it would injure his style. Serious warnings were more than once extended against the influence of that poet. The Judge might have felt still more deeply, had he known the powerful impression that writer had made upon Bryant's mind. "I shall never forget," says Richard H. Dana, " with what feeling my friend Bryant described to me the effect produced upon him by Wordsworth's Ballads." "A thousand springs," he said, "seemed to gush up at once in my heart, — and the face of nature, of a sudden, to change into a strange freshness and life."

Mr. Bryant, in speaking of the "Thanatopsis," stated that, at a time when he was about to leave home, he placed the original copy of that poem, together with some other manuscript poems, in a drawer in his father's office. During his absence, his father met with the papers, and was so much pleased with the " Thanatopsis " that he sent it, without his son's knowledge, to the editors of the " North American Review," that periodical having been recently established. This was in 1817, and thus it was published. At that time only forty-nine of the eighty-one lines existed, and four verses in rhyme prefaced them, which were never intended for such a position. The first sixteen and a half lines and the last fifteen and a half, as they now stand, were afterwards added, and several important alterations also introduced.

Mr. Bryant's brother John was on a visit to the homestead. He was a man of marked ability, and had resided for many years in Illinois. He had much to say of his brother's boyhood ; his precociousness, his individuality, and the manner in which all the young people of that period looked up to him. When he was yet quite a child, his father would offer him a dollar to write verses upon a given subject. John repeated to me some verses which he yet remembered, written in this way. "We all looked up to my brother," he said, "as something wonderful! Oh," he continued, " we thought everything of William."

The father also was very proud of his boy. Mr. Bryant himself says : —

> " he taught my youth
> The art of verse, and in the bud of life
> Offered me to the Muses."

Mrs. Bryant lived eight years after her return from Italy, and in 1866 passed peacefully away, " sustained and soothed by an unfaltering trust." It was a serious blow, but Mr. Bryant met it with that unshaken Christian fortitude, which alone could give support. Instead of becoming crushed, he braced himself for redoubled activity. With extraordinary intellectual vigor, at the age of seventy-one, he commenced, in earnest, the translation of the Iliad. He was at work upon this while I was at Cummington. It occupied regularly a portion of the day, but did not interfere with any domestic enjoyment. He told me he translated from the Greek on an average forty lines a day, and at times double that amount. I was every day in his study, and saw no English translation among his many books. He had a German translation to which he might occasionally refer. He stated that he had always been fond of Greek, and that, when he first acquired the knowledge of that language, a fellow-student, who has since risen to eminence in the law, wept because he could not keep up with him. I took to Mr. Bryant a copy of Felton's Lectures on Greek Literature, which he had not seen, and which interested him. His translation of the Iliad was completed in 1869, after which he at once commenced the Odyssey, which he completed in 1871, making six years in which he was engaged upon the work. Had he executed nothing else, it would have been a monument to his ability ; an achievement, at his period of life, which under the circumstances may be considered unsurpassed.

Thus did Mr. Bryant continue in intellectual vigor to the last ; with every faculty in full strength ; and even his poetic genius and artistic skill unimpaired. At length, on a beautiful day, June 12th, — the very month in which he had most desired to go, — he was suddenly taken from us. His last word was a tribute to the cause of Liberty ; and his closing effort a final demonstration of the exertion he was ever ready to make in behalf of others.

I know of nothing more applicable to the present occasion than Mr. Bryant's hitherto unpublished words in a note which I received from him, on the death of President Quincy, July, 1864. As I read the page, seemingly fresh from his pen, it is as if he were himself speaking : —

" I was about," he writes, " to call it a sad event, but it is so only in a limited sense ; — sad to those who survive, and who shall see his venerable form, and hear his wise and kindly words no more ; but otherwise, no more sad than the close of a well-spent day, or the satisfactory completion of any task which has long occupied our attention. Mr. Quincy, in laying aside the dull weeds of mortality, has with them put off old age with its infirmities, and (passing to a nobler stage of existence) enters again upon the activity of youth, with more exalted powers and more perfect organs. Instead of lamenting his departure at a time of life considerably beyond the common age of man, the generation which now inhabits the earth should give thanks that he has lived so long, and should speak of the blessing of being allowed for so many years to have before them so illustrious an example."

What words could be found more appropriate to himself? I will only add his own eloquent utterance on the death of his friend Washington Irving : " Farewell, thou hast entered into the rest prepared, from the foundation of the world, for serene and gentle spirits like thine. Farewell, happy in thy life, happy in thy death, happier in the reward to which that death was the assured passage. The brightness of that enduring fame, which thou hast won on earth, is but a shadowy symbol of the glory to which thou art admitted in the world beyond the grave."

APPENDIX.

" THOU hast taught us, with delighted eye,
    To gaze upon the mountains, — to behold,
With deep affection, the pure ample sky
    And clouds along its blue abysses rolled,
To love the song of waters, and to hear
The melody of winds with charmèd ear."

3

ANCESTRY.

———◆———

STEPHEN BRYANT, the founder of the Bryant family on this continent, came from England, in the "Mayflower," about 1610. Ichabod Bryant moved from Raynham to West Bridgewater in 1745. His son, Philip Bryant, was born in 1732, and practised medicine in North Bridgewater, Massachusetts; he married a daughter of Dr. Abiel Howard, of Bridgewater. Peter Bryant was born at North Bridgewater, 1767. He studied medicine, and succeeded his father in his profession. He became interested in the daughter of Ebenezer Snell. Mr. Snell removing with his family to Cummington, Peter Bryant soon followed, and was united in marriage to Sarah Snell in 1792. She was a lineal descendant of John Alden, the famous lieutenant of Miles Standish, " the stalwart captain of Plymouth."

The second child of Peter and Sarah Bryant was born November 3, 1794. The name given to this child was WILLIAM CULLEN, in honor of Dr. Cullen, the great medical authority of that time, professor in the University of Edinburgh; and thus the name of the distinguished Scottish physician has become associated with American literature, and rendered familiar as a household word to the whole American people.

WILLIAM CULLEN BRYANT born at Cummington, 3d November, 1794, in early youth wrote various poems which attracted attention and were widely circulated. In 1808, he published a satirical poem entitled "The Embargo, by a Youth of Thirteen." In 1810, at the age of sixteen, he entered Williams College. He took an honorable dismissal in 1812, and commenced the study of law with the Hon. William Baylis, of West Bridgewater. He afterward studied for two years in the office of Judge Howe. In 1815, at the age of twenty-one, he was admitted to the bar. In 1817, his "Thanatopsis" appeared in the "North American Review," which was followed by his "Lines to a Water-fowl." This year he took up his residence at Great Barrington, where he continued until 1825, when he removed to New York, and became the editor of the "New York Review." He delivered his poem on "The Ages" before the Phi Beta Kappa Society of Harvard University in 1821, and the same year he was married to Frances Fairchild. In 1827, he became one of the editors of the "Evening Post," which position he continued to fill for more than half a century, holding the same at the time of his death. In 1864, his seventieth birthday was celebrated by the Century Club, at which the most distinguished literary men of the country were present. In 1866, he was called to severe affliction in the death of his wife, after a most happy union of forty-five years. In his seventy-first year, he commenced the translation of the "Iliad," and of the "Odyssey" in 1870, both of which translations were completed within the space of six years. On the 29th of May, 1878, he delivered an address in Central Park, New York, in honor of the Italian patriot Mazzini. This was his last public act. He fell exhausted, and on the twelfth day of June a nation mourned his departure.

"CHEERFUL HE GAVE HIS BEING UP, AND WENT
TO SHARE THE HOLY REST THAT WAITS A LIFE WELL SPENT."

INCIDENT AT COLLEGE.

—◆—

THE year that Mr. Bryant entered Williams College, " Knicker-bocker's History of New York " made its appearance; and, with his keen appreciation of humor, he became at once so much interested in it, that he committed a portion to memory, to repeat as a declamation before his class.   In the recital, however, he was so completely overcome with laughter, that it became impossible for him to proceed.   He received a rebuke from his tutor, who would have done himself no discredit, if he had laughed also.   Now that seventy years have gone by, are we not, by this little incident, drawn yet more closely to one who, in the youthful sympathy of his nature, felt such a hearty response to the irresistible humor of Knickerbocker?

TWENTY-THREE years after this college experience, Washington Irving, the warm admirer of Bryant, at that time Secretary of the American Legation in London, edited an English edition of Bryant's Poems, with a cordial and flattering Introduction.

AT ROSLYN.

———◆———

" Noiselessly, around,
From perch to perch, the solitary bird
Passes."

Forest Hymn.

" Here build, and dread no harsher sound,
To scare you from the sheltering tree,
Than winds that stir the branches round,
And murmur of the bee."

Return of the Birds.

" Brood, kind creatures ; you need not fear
Thieves and robbers while I am here."

Robert of Lincoln.

AT Roslyn, while we were looking at the trees near the house, I observed a large branch upon one of them sawn nearly off, so that its weight would have quickly brought it to the ground. This result was prevented by ropes interlacing the branches, carefully securing the bough to the main trunk and to the heavier branches above.

Mr. Bryant, seeing that curiosity was awakened, with a smile gave the explanation.

" My gardener," he said, " came to the conclusion that the absence of this bough would be an improvement to the tree. The work of destruction was at once commenced, when his purpose attracted my notice. On that branch," said Mr. Bryant, pointing beneath the leaves, " you will see a nest, where the parent birds had been watching their young. I instantly ordered the gardener to bring ropes and have the branch carefully secured in its place. It was an awkward thing to accomplish ; but he has at least succeeded sufficiently well to leave the birds undisturbed, — which is a great satisfaction, — and this accounts for what you see."

If the " Water-fowl " was unconsciously immortalized, and the " Bob-o'-link " made the subject of attractive thought, these birds, by the same mind, had secured to them their comfortable home, the very existence of which was threatened ; while the act itself was so complete a poem that the author did not need to put it into verse.

A SUNDAY AT CUMMINGTON.

THERE was one incident connected with our visit to Cummington, so characteristic of Mr. Bryant, I am tempted to relate it.

On Friday, he said to me, as we were walking among the fields : " It is my wish that on Sunday we should have religious services in the school-house. There is no church-edifice near at hand, and the school-house will be just the place. I will spread the intelligence among the people, and they will gladly come."

I stated that I had no written discourse with me; and I was not sure that I should be able to meet the wants of the people thus called together. Mr. Bryant replied, no written discourse was needed, that the thought which would naturally present itself could be spoken, and that nothing could be better than to have the simple truths of Christianity brought directly home to the heart.

In replying that I would cheerfully do whatever he desired, I may as well confess that I added, I did not so much mind speaking before the people as before him. " Oh ! " said he, with a sweet smile and a half reproving look, " I should think you had known me long enough not to feel thus. No one will welcome more heartily whatever may be said." " Make any arrangement you please," I said, " and I shall rejoice to be with you."

The next morning, Mr. Bryant and his brother John left home for the school-house, — a picturesque little building, and quite within sight. Here they were to make any needed preparation, and put things in order for the morrow.

It was not long before they returned with a look of disappointment. Something baffled them. What it was they were rather reluctant to communicate. However, they soon made known the fact that the school-house would not answer. The desks were all fixtures, and were intended for young children. Any needed change was wholly impracticable. The impossibility of using that building, for the purpose proposed, was decisive. Our plans seemed to melt before us.

So matters rested. Presently, Mr. Bryant and his brother disappeared, and were no more seen through the whole morning. The poet might be deeply engaged over his translation of Homer. The battles of the Greeks were, perhaps, absorbing his mind. No: the two brothers were away from home, — no one knew where. At length, they returned with an evident look of triumph. " It is all right!" " We have arranged matters to our satisfaction!" Such were their exclamations. The "Homestead," where we were, was midway upon the hill. Some ways up, near to the summit of this elevation, Mr. Bryant was erecting a house for his son-in-law, Parke Godwin, and his family. The building was covered in, but not completed. Carpenters and mechanics were busily at work. The brothers had proceeded thither to investigate. Mr. Bryant was not ready to succumb. He had made up his mind to have a service; and a service there should be!

Why not have it in this new building? The scene looked at present like a chaos, with a clutter of shavings and barrels and boards. This did not matter. The workmen were ordered to clear the place. All hands were soon at work, and the brothers enjoyed it thoroughly. It seemed like old times. They were boys again. They worked with a will. The piles of chips and shavings speedily vanished; all rubbish was soon removed from the whole lower floor. Then the question was for seats. Boxes and barrels were arranged, and boards laid upon them in orderly rows: all this was extemporized in a masterly manner. Every difficulty was overcome, and in due time a most primitive place of worship was completed, reminding one of the Covenanters and the Puritans; though this was a cathedral compared to places where they often met. The scene around was certainly grand, — the wide sweep of valleys and the vast amphitheatre of wooded hills.

We now waited for the morrow, which soon came, — a calm September morning. The population was widely scattered. There was no village in the immediate neighborhood. Simple farm-houses appeared here and there, humble homes under the shadow of spreading trees. Word had been spread from dwelling to dwelling, and farmers with their families were seen upon the way. Aged people were there with whom the journey of life was nearly ended, and little children in their Sunday clothes. Invalids, feeble and worn, who were seldom out, and mothers with their infants in their arms. Then there were strong sunburnt laborers and young men in the vigor of life. The new house was soon thronged. All the seats were occupied. Some of the young people were seated upon the stairs, and some stood by the open windows. Familiar hymns were sung to tunes in which all could unite. It was, in fact, a most touching and beautiful sight, — thoroughly earnest and good. I doubt if the sun shone that day upon a truer or happier body of worshippers, and among them all, perhaps, no one enjoyed it more truly than Mr. Bryant.

When the services were ended, there were friendly greetings. Mr. Bryant appeared like a father in the midst of his family. All wished and received a pleasant word or look, and evidently valued it as a patriarchal benediction. Thus closed an occasion not soon by any present to be forgotten.

JOHN HOWARD BRYANT, a younger brother of William, was born at Cummington, 22d July, 1807. In youth, while at the Rensselaer school at Troy, he excelled in Mathematics and the Natural Sciences. In 1831, at the age of twenty-four, he emigrated to the West, establishing himself at Princeton, Illinois. At one time he was representative in the State Legislature. Communications from his pen have appeared at various times in leading periodicals. In 1855, a volume of his poems, from the press of his brother William, was published by the Appletons, which was favorably received by the public.

WHILE at Cummington, being one morning alone with Mr. Bryant in his library, he said, "Some of my brother's poems have great merit;" and taking up a copy of the volume from the table, in which John had written, "For the Old Homestead," Mr. Bryant said, "Let me read to you." He commenced one of the poems, but before proceeding far his voice became tremulous; more and more he was overcome by emotion; until no longer able to read, he handed me the book, saying, "Excuse me, — I cannot go on, — please read it yourself."

Under a calm and unimpassioned manner, there was in Mr. Bryant's nature hidden depths of feeling; and this tribute to his brother has often come to my recollection, as an instance of his own sensibility, and a proof of the strong bond which united the brothers.

BEFORE my leaving Cummington, Mr. Bryant wrote his name, as a token of remembrance, in a volume of his Poems, adding the closing verse of his well-known lines to the water-fowl : —

> " He who, from zone to zone,
>   Guides through the boundless sky thy certain flight,
> *In the long way that I must tread alone,*
>   *Will lead my steps aright.*"

These words, which had then deep significance, are yet more impressive now.

———◆———

THE COMMUNION-SERVICE AT NAPLES.

THE seven persons who were gathered together at Naples, on that beautiful morning in the spring of 1858, were Mr. and Mrs. Bryant, their daughter Julia and her friend Estelle Ives, Mr. and Mrs. Waterston and their daughter Helen. The rite of baptism was also administered to Julia Bryant and Estelle Ives (now Mrs. Mackie, of Great Barrington). The three young people united with Mr. Bryant in partaking of the Holy Communion for the first time.

Helen Ruthven Waterston, to whom Mr. Bryant paid so exquisite a tribute in one of his " Letters from Spain," was in the bloom of her youth and beauty. An illness soon followed ; and, on the 25th of July, — three months from the day and hour of that hallowed service, — her spirit passed away, on a peaceful Sunday morning. As will be readily understood, such tender associations united us all together by very sacred ties.

WILLIAM C. BRYANT AND RICHARD H. DANA.

———•◦•———

WHEN the "Thanatopsis," and lines " To a Water-fowl," were sent to the editors of the "North American Review," they were sent by Dr. Bryant, the father, anonymously. It was not even stated that they were by the same person. The editing of the periodical was under the special charge of Richard H. Dana and Professor Channing. These poems were placed in the hands of Mr. Dana. After reading them, he said, " I do not think these poems were written by an American." " Why so?" was the response. " I do not know of any American," replied Mr. Dana, "who could have written them."

This statement was made to me by Mr. Dana himself, who had the fullest appreciation of the remarkable character of the productions. He was eager to welcome this new compeer into the world of letters. His curiosity was aroused; and, when informed that the name of the writer was Bryant, who was then a member of the Massachusetts Legislature, Mr. Dana (residing at that time in Cambridge) at once came into the city, and repaired to the State House, where the Representative, Dr. Peter Bryant, from Cummington, was pointed out. Mr. Dana told me he looked upon the gentleman designated with deep interest. He saw a man of striking presence, but the stamp of genius was wanting; and, with unfeigned disappointment, he said, " That is a good head, but I do not see the ' Thanatopsis ' there ! "

This exclamation, so remarkable for penetration and originality, was characteristic of Mr. Dana's sagacious judgment. He could recognize genius, he was ready and anxious to extend a cordial salutation ; but he was convinced that, in the decision here made, he had judged rightly.

At no distant day, the two kindred minds came together, differing, yet harmonious ; when immediately a friendship was formed, which, amid the vicissitudes of half a century, proved indissoluble.

Mr. Dana is yet with us, in the ripeness of years, all his faculties strong and vigorous. Long may Providence spare him, to be unto many a counsellor and a friend.

" On my heart
Deeply hath sunk the lesson thou hast given,
And shall not soon depart."

FOUR verses were printed in the "North American Review," as an introduction to the "Thanatopsis." . It was never intended by Mr. Bryant that they should thus have been published. They were sent, through mistake, by his father, with the manuscript of "Thanatopsis." They were originally written as a separate production; as such, they are worth preserving. They have never been included by Mr. Bryant in any collected edition of his Poems; but they are interesting from their history, and as the expression of his views in the earlier period of life: —

Not that from life, and all its woes,
  The hand of death shall set me free;
Not that this head shall then repose
  In the low vale most peacefully.

Ah ! when I touch Time's farthest brink,
  A kinder solace must attend:
It chills my very soul to think
  On the dread hour when life must end.

In vain the flattering verse may breathe
  Of ease from pain and rest from strife;
There is a sacred dread of death
  Inwoven with the strings of life.

This bitter cup at first was given,
  When angry Justice frowned severe;
And 'tis the eternal doom of Heaven
  That man must view the grave with fear.

Through what Mr. Bryant has written at successive periods of life, we can see that his mind was more and more illumined by an exalted Christian faith. In the following verses, Christ, risen and glorified, opens to the view visions of heaven : —

JESUS OF NAZARETH.

" I shall not die, but live."

All praise to Him of Nazareth,
  The Holy One who came,
For love of man, to die a death
  Of agony and shame.

Dark was the grave ; but since He lay
  Within its dreary cell,
The beams of Heaven's eternal day
  Upon its threshold dwell.

He grasped the iron veil; He drew
  Its gloomy folds aside,
And opened to his followers' view
  The glorious world they hide.

———————

What unspeakable consolation breathes through every word of the following verses! How many anxious and sorrowing hearts have here found comfort and peace!

BLESSED ARE THEY THAT MOURN.

Deem not that they are blessed alone
  Whose days a peaceful tenor keep;
The God, who loves our race, has shown
  A blessing for the eyes that weep.

The light of smiles shall fill again
  The lids that overflow with tears;
And weary hours of woe and pain
  Are promises of happier years.

There is a day of sunny rest
  For every dark and troubled night:
And Grief may bide an evening guest;
  But Joy shall come with early light.

And thou, who, o'er thy friend's low bier,
  Dost shed the bitter drops like rain,
Hope that a brighter, happier sphere
  Will give him to thy arms again.

Nor let the good man's trust depart,
  Though life its common gifts deny;
Though, with a pierced and bleeding heart,
  And spurned of men, he goes to die.

For God hath marked each sorrowing day,
  And numbered every secret tear,
And heaven's long age of bliss shall pay
  For all his children suffer here.

AGAIN, in his lines on " Waiting by the Gate," he says : —

Some approach the threshold whose looks are blank with fear,
And some whose temples brighten with joy in drawing near,
As if they saw dear faces, and caught the gracious eye
Of Him, the Sinless Teacher, who came for us to die.

I mark the joy, the terror; yet these within my heart,
Can neither wake the dread nor the longing to depart;
And, in the sunshine streaming on quiet wood and lea,
I stand and calmly wait, till the hinges turn for me.

M R. BRYANT, in a private note, — quoted in the remarks, — dated Roslyn, July 7th, 1864, — while speaking of the death of President Quincy, who had just departed this life, in his ninety-third year, says, " Mr. Quincy *has put off old age* with all its infirmities, and (passing to a nobler stage of existence) *enters again upon the activity of youth*, with more exalted powers and more perfect organs."

This inspiring thought was with Mr. Bryant more than a poetic imagination, it was a living faith, a deep and abiding conviction. He has given exquisite expression to the same sublime idea in his verses entitled " The Return of Youth."

This poem, we think, may be counted among the most perfect productions of Mr. Bryant's genius. The grand idea of immortality, here presented, not only robs the grave of its terror, but lifts the thought triumphantly to realms of celestial splendor; not vague and unreal, but natural and homelike; kindling in the mind an almost infinite longing. He addresses a friend who is sorrowing over the loss of his golden prime, the youthful years which have taken flight only too soon, while the shadows of time are swiftly falling. " Look not," exclaims the Poet, " with despair to the Past, but, with glowing anticipation, gaze into the Future ! "

THE RETURN OF YOUTH.

Oh, grieve thou not, nor think thy youth is gone,
   Nor deem that glorious season e'er could die :
Thy pleasant youth, a little while withdrawn,
   Waits on the horizon of a brighter sky;
Waits, like the Morn, that folds her wings and hides
   Till the slow stars bring back her dawning hour;
Waits, like the vanished Spring, that slumbering bides
   Her own sweet time to waken bud and flower.

There shall he welcome thee, when thou shalt stand
   On his bright morning hills, with smiles more sweet
Than when at first he took thee by the hand,
   Through the fair earth to lead thy tender feet.
He shall bring back, but brighter, broader still,
   Life's early glory to thine eyes again,
Shall clothe thy spirit with new strength, and fill
   Thy leaping heart with warmer love than then.

Hast thou not glimpses, in the twilight here,
    Of mountains where immortal morn prevails?
Comes there not, through the silence, to thine ear
    A gentle rustling of the morning gales ;
A murmur, wafted from that glorious shore,
    Of streams that water banks for ever fair,
And voices of the loved ones gone before,
    More musical in that celestial air?

NATURALLY was it remembered, when Mr. Bryant's spirit passed quietly away on a beautiful day in June, that it was in accordance with his expressed wish ; and many fondly repeated what he had written years ago, and felt that Providence had kindly heard and answered his prayer.

I thought that when I came to lie
    At rest within the ground,
'Twere pleasant, that in flowery June,
When brooks send up a cheerful tune
    And groves a joyous sound,
The sexton's hand, my grave to make,
The rich, green mountain-turf should break.

*   *   *   *   *   *   *

Blue be the sky and soft the breeze,
    Earth green beneath the feet,
And be the damp mould gently pressed
Into my narrow place of rest.

There through the long, long summer hours,
    The golden light should lie,
And thick young herbs and groups of flowers
    Stand in their beauty by :
The oriole should build and tell
His love-tale close beside my cell.

And when we think of the last service at Roslyn, and of that peaceful resting-place by the side of his beloved wife, amid scenes so long familiar, we may well continue to repeat his words, —

" And what if cheerful shouts at noon
　　Come from the village sent,
Or song of maids, beneath the moon,
　　With fairy laughter blent?
And what if in the evening light
Betrothèd lovers walk in sight
　　Of my low monument?
I would the lovely scene around
Might know no sadder sight nor sound.

And if, around my place of sleep,
The friends I love should come to weep,
　　They might not haste to go ;
Soft airs, and song, and light, and bloom
Should keep them lingering by my tomb."

Thus was it that his wish, like a presentiment, was to be fulfilled ; and when that event, so prefigured, arrived, literally true to his own words, he went

　　" Like one who wraps the drapery of his couch
　　About him, and lies down to pleasant dreams."

And even more fully does he depict his entrance upon the Great Future, when in his " Journey of Life," he says, —

" — I, with faltering footsteps, journey on,
Watching the stars that roll the hours away,
　Till the faint light, that guides me now, is gone,
And, like another life, the glorious day
Shall open o'er me, from the empyreal height,
WITH WARMTH, and CERTAINTY, and BOUNDLESS LIGHT."

　　" Even then he trod
　The threshold of the world unknown ;
　　Already, from the seat of God,
　A ray upon his garments shone."

" Why weep ye then for him, who, having won
     The bound of man's appointed years, at last,
 Life's blessings all enjoyed, life's labors done,
     Serenely to his final rest has passed;
 While the soft memory of his virtues, yet,
 Lingers like twilight hues, when the bright sun is set? "

POETICAL TRIBUTES

TO

FRANCES F. BRYANT,

BY

WILLIAM CULLEN BRYANT.

———◆———

Written at Various Seasons,

THROUGH MANY YEARS OF DEVOTED AFFECTION.

THESE poems, addressed to Mrs. Bryant, are reprinted from Mr. Bryant's collected works, partly as a tribute to her memory, and in part that they may stand together and be so read. As usually printed, the reader might not necessarily associate them with Mrs. Bryant; for instance, in the lines headed "The Twenty-seventh of March," no mention is made that this was the birthday of Mrs. Bryant. These lines, for several years, like other tributes to her, were retained in manuscript, and held as too private and sacred for general publication. Mrs. Bryant's unaffected modesty shrunk from publicity, which was doubtless the reason why the name was originally withheld; but now that she has entered into that state of being where they are in heavenly companionship, it is pleasant to bring these unsurpassed expressions together, as the utterance of a love that knew no change save that it grew deeper and stronger as the years wore away.

OH, FAIREST OF THE RURAL MAIDS.

This poem, addressed by Mr. Bryant to Frances Fairchild, was written amid the beautiful scenery of Great Barrington early in that acquaintance which led to their union in 1821, — the same year in which his poem of "The Ages" was given before the Phi Beta Kappa Society, at Cambridge.

OH, fairest of the rural maids !
    Thy birth was in the forest shades;
Green boughs, and glimpses of the sky,
Were all that met thine infant eye.

Thy sports, thy wanderings, when a child,
Were ever in the sylvan wild ;
And all the beauty of the place
Is in thy heart, and on thy face.

The twilight of the trees and rocks
Is in the light shade of thy locks ;
Thy step is in the wind, that weaves
Its playful way among the leaves.

Thine eyes are springs, in whose serene
And silent waters heaven is seen;
Their lashes are the herbs that look
On their young figures in the brook.

The forest depths, by foot unpressed,
Are not more sinless than thy breast ;
The holy peace, that fills the air
Of those calm solitudes, is there.

THE TWENTY-SEVENTH OF MARCH.

Mrs. Bryant's birthday.   Written March, 1855

On, gentle one, thy birthday sun should rise
Amid a chorus of the merriest birds
That ever sang the stars out of the sky
In a June morning.   Rivulets should send
A voice of gladness from their winding paths,
Deep in o'erarching grass, where playful winds,
Stirring the loaded stems, should shower the dew
Upon the glassy water.   Newly blown
Roses, by thousands, to the garden walks
Should tempt the loitering moth and diligent bee.
The longest, brightest day in all the year
Should be the day on which thy cheerful eyes
First opened on the earth, to make thy haunts
Fairer and gladder for thy kindly looks.

Thus might a poet say ; but I must bring
A birthday offering of an humbler strain,
And yet it may not please thee less.   I hold
That 'twas the fitting season for thy birth
When March, just ready to depart, begins
To soften into April.   Then we have
The delicatest and most welcome flowers,
And yet they take least heed of bitter wind
And lowering sky.   The periwinkle then,
In an hour's sunshine, lifts her azure blooms
Beside the cottage-door ; within the woods
Tufts of ground-laurel, creeping underneath
The leaves of the last summer, send their sweets
Up to the chilly air, and, by the oak,
The squirrel-cups, a graceful company,
Hide in their bells a soft aërial blue —
Sweet flowers, that nestle in the humblest nooks,
And yet within whose smallest bud is wrapt
A world of promise!   Still the north wind breathes
His frost, and still the sky sheds snow and sleet ;
Yet ever, when the sun looks forth again,
The flowers smile up to him from their low seats.

Well hast thou borne the bleak March day of life.
Its storms and its keen winds to thee have been
Most kindly tempered, and through all its gloom
There has been warmth and sunshine in thy heart;
The griefs of life to thee have been like snows,
That light upon the fields in early spring,
Making them greener.   In its milder hours,
The smile of this pale season, thou hast seen
The glorious bloom of June, and in the note
Of early bird, that comes a messenger
From climes of endless verdure, thou hast heard
The choir that fills the summer woods with song.
Now be the hours that yet remain to thee
Stormy or sunny, sympathy and love,
That inextinguishably dwell within
Thy heart, shall give a beauty and a light
To the most desolate moments, like the glow
Of a bright fireside in the wildest day;
And kindly words and offices of good
Shall wait upon thy steps, as thou goest on,
Where God shall lead thee, till thou reach the gates
Of a more genial season, and thy path
Be lost to human eye among the bowers
And living fountains of a brighter land.

THE FUTURE LIFE.

Written in 1837.

How shall I know thee in the sphere which keeps
   The disembodied spirits of the dead ;
When all of thee that time could wither sleeps
   And perishes among the dust we tread?

For I shall feel the sting of ceaseless pain
   If there I meet thy gentle presence not ;
Nor hear the voice I love, nor read again
   In thy serenest eyes the tender thought.

Will not thy own meek heart demand me there ?
   That heart whose fondest throbs to me were given —
My name on earth was ever in thy prayer,
   And wilt thou never utter it in heaven?

In meadows fanned by heaven's life-breathing wind,
  In the resplendence of that glorious sphere,
And larger movements of the unfettered mind,
  Wilt thou forget the love that joined us here?

The love that lived through all the stormy past,
  And meekly with my harsher nature bore,
And deeper grew, and tenderer to the last,
  Shall it expire with life, and be no more?

A happier lot than mine, and larger light,
  Await thee there, for thou hast bowed thy will
In cheerful homage to the rule of right,
  And lovest all, and renderest good for ill.

For me, the sordid cares in which I dwell
  Shrink and consume my heart, as heat the scroll;
And wrath has left its scar — that fire of hell
  Has left its frightful scar upon my soul.

Yet, though thou wear'st the glory of the sky,
  Wilt thou not keep the same beloved name,
The same fair thoughtful brow, and gentle eye,
  Lovelier in heaven's sweet climate, yet the same?

Shalt thou not teach me, in that calmer home,
  The wisdom that I learned so ill in this —
The wisdom which is love — till I become
  Thy fit companion in that land of bliss?

THE CLOUD ON THE WAY.

SEE before us, in our journey, broods a mist upon the ground;
Thither leads the path we walk in, blending with that gloomy bound.
Never eye hath pierced its shadows to the mystery they screen;
Those who once have passed within it never more on earth are seen.
Now it seems to stoop beside us, now at seeming distance lowers,
Leaving banks that tempt us onward bright with summer-green and
  flowers.

Yet it blots the way for ever ; there our journey ends at last ;
Into that dark cloud we enter, and are gathered to the past.
Thou who, in this flinty pathway, leading through a stranger-land,
Passest down the rocky valley, walking with me hand in hand,
Which of us shall be the soonest folded to that dim Unknown?
Which shall leave the other walking in this flinty path alone?
Even now I see thee shudder, and thy cheek is white with fear,
And thou clingest to my side — as comes that darkness sweeping near.
" Here," thou say'st, " the path is rugged, sown with thorns that wound
        the feet ;
But the sheltered glens are lovely, and the rivulet's song is sweet ;
Roses breathe from tangled thickets ; lilies bend from ledges brown ;
Pleasantly between the pelting showers the sunshine gushes down ;
Dear are those who walk beside us, they whose looks and voices make
All this rugged region cheerful, till I love it for their sake.
Far be yet the hour that takes me where that chilly shadow lies,
From the things I know and love, and from the sight of loving eyes."
So thou murmurest, fearful one : but see, we tread a rougher way ;
Fainter glow the gleams of sunshine, that upon the dark rocks play;
Rude winds strew the faded flowers upon the crags o'er which we pass :
Banks of verdure, when we reach them, hiss with tufts of withered grass.
One by one we miss the voices which we loved so well to hear;
One by one the kindly faces in that shadow disappear.
Yet upon the mist before us fix thine eyes with closer view;
See, beneath its sullen skirts, the rosy morning glimmers through.
One whose feet the thorns have wounded, passed that barrier and came
        back,
With a glory on His footsteps lighting yet the dreary track.
Boldly enter where He entered : all that seems but darkness here,
When thou hast passed beyond it, haply shall be crystal-clear.
Viewed from that serener realm, the walks of human life may lie,
Like the page of some familiar volume, open to thine eye;
Haply, from the overhanging shadow, thou may'st stretch an unseen
        hand,
To support the wavering steps that print with blood the rugged land.
Haply, leaning o'er the pilgrim, all unweeting thou art near,
Thou may'st whisper words of warning or of comfort to his ear,
Till, beyond the border where that brooding mystery bars the sight,
Those whom thou hast fondly cherished stand with thee in peace and
        light.

THE LIFE THAT IS.

Written at Castellamare, after Mrs. Bryant's recovery from illness in Naples,
May, 1858.

THOU, who so long hast pressed the couch of pain,
   Oh, welcome, welcome back to life's free breath; —
To life's free breath and day's sweet light again,
   From the chill shadows of the gate of death :

For thou hadst reached the twilight bound between
   The world of spirits and this grosser sphere;
Dimly by thee the things of earth were seen,
   And faintly fell earth's voices on thine ear.

And now, how gladly we behold, at last,
   The wonted smile returning to thy brow;
The very wind's low whisper breathing past,
   In the light leaves, is music to thee now.

Thou wert not weary of thy lot; the earth
   Was ever good and pleasant in thy sight;
Still clung thy loves about the household hearth;
   And sweet was every day's returning light.

Then welcome back to all thou would'st not leave,
   To this grand march of seasons, days, and hours;
The glory of the morn, the glow of eve,
   The beauty of the streams, and stars, and flowers;

To eyes on which thine own delight to rest;
   To voices which it is thy joy to hear;
To the kind toils that ever pleased thee best,
   The willing tasks of love, that made life dear.

Welcome to grasp of friendly hands; to prayers
   Offered where crowds in reverent worship come;
Or softly breathed amid the tender cares
   And loving inmates of thy quiet home.

Thou bring'st no tidings of the better land,
   Even from its verge; the mys'cries opened there
Are what the faithful heart may understand
   In its still depths, yet words may not declare.

And well I deem, that, from the brighter side
  Of life's dim border, some o'erflowing rays,
Streamed from the inner glory, shall abide
  Upon thy spirit through the coming days.

Twice wert thou given me ; once in thy fair prime,
  Fresh from the fields of youth, when first we met,
And all the blossoms of that hopeful time
  Clustered and glowed where'er thy steps were set.

And now, in thy ripe autumn, once again
  Given back to fervent prayers and yearnings strong,
From the drear realm of sickness and of pain,
  When we had watched, and feared, and trembled long.

Now may we keep thee from the balmy air
  And radiant walks of heaven a little space,
Where He, who went before thee to prepare
  For His meek followers, shall assign thy place.

T. H. James

The Wooden Bowl

ISBN/EAN: 9783744708357

Printed in Europe, USA, Canada, Australia, Japan

Cover: Foto ©Thomas Meinert / pixelio.de

More available books at **www.hansebooks.com**

JAPANESE FAIRY TALE SERIES. No. 16.

THE WOODEN BOWL.

Told in English by

Mrs. T. H. James.

土佐又兵衛筆

日本昔噺

第十六號

ジエイムス夫人 譯述

東京市 佐柄木町

弘文社發兌

          " Death should come
       Gently, to one of gentle mould like thee,
As light winds wandering through groves of bloom
       Detach the delicate blossoms from the tree.
Close thy sweet eyes, calmly, and without pain;
And we will trust in God to see thee yet again."

MR. BRYANT'S LAST ADDRESS,

IN THE

CENTRAL PARK, NEW YORK,

29TH OF MAY, 1878.

———◆———

> "Man foretells afar
> The courses of the stars; — the very hour
> He knows when they shall darken or grow bright;
>
>   *   *   *   *   *
>
> Yet doth the eclipse of sorrow and of death
> Come unforewarned!"

Extracts from Mr. Bryant's Address in the Central Park, 29th May, 1878.

ON UNVEILING THE BUST OF MAZZINI, THE ITALIAN STATESMAN.

HISTORY, my friends, has recorded the deeds of Mazzini on a tablet which will endure while the annals of Italy are read. To-day a bust is unveiled which will make millions familiar with the Divine image stamped on the countenance of one of the greatest men of our times.

The idea of Italian unity and liberty was the passion of Mazzini's life. It took possession of him in youth; it grew stronger as the years went on, and lost none of its power over him in his age. Nor is it at all surprising that it should have taken a strong hold on his youthful imagination.

I recollect very well that when, forty-four years ago, I first entered Italy, — then held down under the weight of a score of despotisms, — the same idea forcibly suggested itself to my mind as I looked southward from the slopes of the mountain country. There lay a great sisterhood of provinces, requiring only a confederate republican government to raise them to the rank of a great power, presenting to the world a single majestic front, and parcelling out the powers of local legislation and government among the different neighborhoods in such a manner as to educate the whole population in a knowledge of the duties and rights of freemen. There were the industrious Piedmontese, the enterprising Genoese, among whom Mazzini was born, — a countryman of Columbus; there were the ambitious Venetians and the Lombards, rejoicing in their fertile plains; and there, as the imagination followed the ridge of the Apennines toward the Strait of Messina, were the Tuscans, famed in letters; the Umbrians, wearing in their aspect the tokens of Latin descent; the Romans, in their centre of arts; the gay Neapolitans; and, further south, the versatile Sicilians, over whose valleys rolls the smoke of the most famous volcano in the world.

As we traverse these regions in thought, we recognize them all as parts of one Italy, yet each inhabited by Italians of a different character from the rest; all speaking Italian, but with a difference in each province; each region cherishing its peculiar traditions, which reach back to the beginning of civilization, and its usages observed for ages.

Well might the great man, whose bust we at this time disclose to the public gaze, be deeply moved by this spectacle of his countrymen and kindred bound in the shackles of a brood of local tyrannies which kept them apart, that they might with more ease be oppressed.

When he further considered the many great men who had risen from time to time in Italy as examples of the intellectual endowments of her people, — statesmen, legislators, men of letters, men eminent in philosophy, in arms, and in arts, — I say that he might well claim for his birthplace of such men the unity of its provinces to make it great, and the liberty of its people to raise them up to the standard of their mental endowments. Who shall blame him — who in this land of freedom — for demanding in behalf of such a country a political constitution framed on the most liberal pattern which the world has seen?

For such a constitution he planned; for that he labored; that object he never suffered to be out of sight. No proclaimer of a new religion was ever more faithful to his mission.

Here, where we have lately closed a sanguinary but successful war in defence of the unity of the States which form our Republic; here, where we have just broken the chains of three millions of bondsmen, is, above all others, the place where a memorial of the great champion of Italian unity and liberty should be set up amid a storm of acclamation from a multitude of freemen.

Yet, earnestly as he desired these ends, and struggled to attain them, the struggle was a noble and manly one. He disdained to compass these ends by base or ferocious means.

*　　*　　*　　*　　*　　*　　*

There was no trial he would not endure, no sacrifice, no labor he would not undertake, no danger he would not encounter, for the sake of that dream of his youth and pursuit of his manhood, — the unity and liberty of Italy.

The country is now united under one political head, save a portion arbitrarily and unjustly added to France; and to the public opinion formed in Italy by the teachings of Mazzini, the union is in large measure due. Italy has now a constitutional government, the best feature of which it owes to the principles of republicanism, in which Mazzini trained a whole generation of the young men of Italy, however short the present government of the country may fall of the ideal standard at which he aimed.

One great result for which he labored was the perfect freedom of religious worship. Well has he deserved the honors of posterity who, holding enforced worship to be an abomination in the sight of God, took his life in his hand and went boldly forward, until the yoke of the great tyranny exercised over the religious conscience in his native country was broken. Such a hero deserves a monument in a land where the government knows no distinction between the religious denominations, and leaves their worship to their consciences.

I will not say that he whose image is to-day unveiled was prudent in all his proceedings : nobody is ; timidity itself is not always prudence. But wherever he went, and whatever he did, he was a power on earth. He wielded an immense influence over men's minds ; he controlled a vast agency, he made himself the centre of a wide diffusion of opinions ; his footsteps are seen in the track of history by those who do not always reflect by whose feet they were impressed.

Such was the celerity of his movements, and so sure the attachment of his followers, that he was the terror of the crowned heads of Europe. Kings trembled when they heard that he had suddenly disappeared from London, and breathed more freely when they learned that he was in his grave. In proportion as he was dreaded, he was maligned.

Image of the illustrious champion of civil and religious liberty, cast in enduring bronze to typify the imperishable renown of thy original! Remain for ages yet to come where we place thee, in this resort of millions. Remain till the day shall dawn — far distant though it be — when the rights and duties of human brotherhood shall be acknowledged by all the races of mankind.

Such were Mr. Bryant's last public words.

Extract from Harper's Monthly for August, 1878.

ON THE DEATH OF WILLIAM CULLEN BRYANT.

THERE was a mournful propriety in the circumstances of the death of Bryant. He was stricken just as he had discharged a characteristic duty with all the felicity for which he was noted; and he was, probably, never wholly conscious from that moment. Happily, we may believe that he was sensible of no decay, and his intimate friends had noted little. He was hale, erect, and strong to the last. All his life a lover of nature and an advocate of liberty, he stood under the trees, on a bright spring day, and paid an eloquent tribute to a devoted servant of liberty in another land, and, while his words yet lingered in the ears of those who heard him, he passed from human sight.

There is, probably, no eminent man in the country upon whose life, and genius, and career the verdict of his fellow-citizens would be more immediate and unanimous.

His character and life had a simplicity and austerity of outline that had become universally familiar, like a neighboring mountain or sea.

His convictions were very strong, and his temper uncompromising. He was independent beyond most Americans. Bryant carried with him the mien and the atmosphere of antique public virtue. He seemed a living embodiment of that simplicity and severity and dignity which we associate with the old republics. A wise stranger would have called him a man nurtured in republican and upon republican traditions.

53

Extract from Scribner's Monthly for August, 1878.

ON THE DEATH OF WILLIAM CULLEN BRYANT.

NOTHING can be purer, nothing more natural, nothing more enduring than his reputation; for it was based in real genius, genuine character, and legitimate achievement.

In his own personal character and history he associated probity with genius, purity with art, and the sweetest Christianity with the highest culture.

He was a great man every way, — great in his gifts, great in his religious faith, great in his works, great in his symmetry, great in his practical handling of the things of personal, social, and political life. Great in his experience of life, great in his wisdom, great in his goodness and sweetness, and great in his modesty and simplicity.

We know of no man dying in America who has been worthier than he of public eulogies and public monuments. We know of nothing more creditable to his countrymen than the universal respect that has been paid to his memory.

"The earth may ring, from shore to shore,
  With echoes of a glorious name;
But he, whose loss our tears deplore,
  Has left behind him, — more than fame."

THE funeral services took place June 14, at All Souls' Church, where Mr. Bryant, through many years, had been a constant attendant and honored member. The services were read by the pastor, Rev. Dr. Bellows, who delivered the funeral address.

The body was then carried to Roslyn, and laid in its last resting-place, by the side of his wife, while a company of little children gathered around the grave, placing upon it flowers as a tribute of respect and affection.

"One by one we miss the voices which we loved so well to hear;
One by one the kindly faces in the shadow disappear."